PASTORS INHERITANCE
THE DEVIL'S
PLAY GROUND

PATRICK W VILLANUEVA

authorHOUSE®

AuthorHouse™
1663 Liberty Drive
Bloomington, IN 47403
www.authorhouse.com
Phone: 833-262-8899

Published by AuthorHouse   02/22/2023

ISBN: 979-8-8230-0162-5 (sc)
ISBN: 979-8-8230-0163-2 (e)

Print information available on the last page.

Any people depicted in stock imagery provided by Getty Images are models, and such images are being used for illustrative purposes only.
Certain stock imagery © Getty Images.

This book is printed on acid-free paper.

Because of the dynamic nature of the Internet, any web addresses or links contained in this book may have changed since publication and may no longer be valid. The views expressed in this work are solely those of the author and do not necessarily reflect the views of the publisher, and the publisher hereby disclaims any responsibility for them.

CONTENTS

PREFACE

As a child of pastoral parents, a licensed minister, the husband of a formidable wife, and the parents of four wonderful sons and two beautiful daughters, I've had a few years to reflect on who I am and how I am becoming the person God intended me to be as He takes me from glory to glory (2 Corinthians 3:18).

Now, as I see my children growing up, I can reflect on my past and how I was taught by my parents our past and present church's beliefs and the strengths and weaknesses of both when it comes to what God calls inheritances (Psalm 127:3). God's Word is always correct; therefore, one must put full reliance on the Word of God, with the Holy Ghost as the teacher. It is the false interpretation or lack of balance (Hebrews 12:28–29; 1 John 4:8,16) that leads to hurt and devastation.

I believe the inheritance, in many cases, is being sold for a bowl of lentils. Pastors and leaders are often so busy "saving the world" that their own children (their inheritance) are being neglected. The enemy is having a proverbial heyday with them. We are more worried about how we look than what we have lost.

The expectation of PKs (preachers' kids) is greater than the protection upon them. Even at the beginning of time, the devil's target was Eve (Genesis 3:1) because he knew she was inexperienced and his best chance of success. In the case of Job, the story reveals, again, that the children were a target to get to the righteous man, Job (Job 1:18–19). This tactic is not new but seems to be the devil's tool, his ploy, his consistent method of operation (1 Peter 5:8–9).

I have learned to make the best of my upbringing, taking my parents' strengths and learning from their mistakes. I am handling church responsibilities to increase protection in raising my children in a society that continues to deteriorate, as the Bible foretells in these last days (2 Timothy 3:1). I believe our children should be ten times greater than who we are. Our mistakes and weaknesses should not be theirs. Every generation should get better, more discerning, more acquainted with God's laws and better equipped to combat the enemy's snares.

Deuteronomy 6:7 tells us to inculcate God's words in our children, to speak of God while we sit or walk, which means all the time! A cover over our inheritance in good and bad times is a must. We give up on our inheritance far too quickly; we often cast them aside like pocket lint.

Our inheritance is being attacked because of our position. The devil is harming our children to hinder their future, who they are destined to be. All thanks to Jesus, for the assurance that He will never leave us nor forsake us, He will always turn it around for our *good* (Hebrews 13:5).

This book contains eye-opening thoughts on how spiritual

leaders spend vast amounts of time with the adult flocks of their churches while their children are left with limited spiritual covering.

Pastors and leaders, you can be great servants of God yet not-so-great *parents*!

Tell the truth and shame the devil!

CHILDHOOD INNOCENCE

I was born in Michigan, a child of Mexican and American descent, in a time that I remember as turbulent. I recall violent riots and lots of racism. I do not remember many children of Spanish descent in my neighborhood, but as kids, we learned to adapt and have fun with whomever and whatever we had to play with. Whenever we left the house, my dad made sure we knew that we stuck together and never left anyone behind, no matter what.

For the most part of living in the middle of Saginaw, Michigan, my four brothers and I spent time riding bikes and repairing and making chopper bikes, like they did on the cartoon *Wheelie and the Chopper Bunch*. Many times we played crash-up derby. As the old saying goes, "Boys will be boys." Thankfully, none of us were hurt badly.

I walked several blocks to buy doughnuts with my brothers, and during one of these ventures we witnessed a man knock down a woman and snatch her purse, spilling her groceries all over the ground.

On other occasions, one of my older brothers bought a big bag of Doritos and poured a whole bottle of Texas Pete hot sauce in the bag and ate them. As kids, we held a race on who could drink a bottle of hot sauce the fastest! This explains why I've moved up in heat to tabasco today.

I was the youngest boy of the family, so my impression of my early years is based on running with my brothers. I don't remember much from that time of my older or younger sister.

My parents were preachers of righteousness, instilling God's laws in us from the start. I remember worship services where the Holy Ghost fell, and people would be slain in the spirit, lying everywhere on the floors! I heard a language that sounded like gibberish at the time (1 Corinthians 13:1 KJV). At times, one person would become loudest, and everything else would become silent until real words were spoken.

My oldest brother played the guitar and sang songs, and my oldest sister played the guitar too. I don't remember my second oldest brother doing much, ministry wise, but he did raise mean dogs for protection! My next oldest brother played the bass guitar and trumpet. My brother just above me didn't play any instruments, to my knowledge. My youngest sister could sing from the early age of two. Then there was me, who learned to play air guitar!

We used to go to an older Caucasian man's house and shoot his BB gun at bottles, and I was called eagle-eyed because I was quite good! Most of all, I loved God from an early age.

During my childhood, my parents traveled for camp meetings and revivals quite often, so much so that my younger sister and I had to travel with them. I slept on chairs, as the services lasted all day and into the night. God's Word was expounded upon by several speakers throughout the day and into the evening, but of course we got the chance to eat lunch and dinner.

Being immersed in godly activities turned out to be a blessing. It was a handicap for many years, and because my parents spent so much time in ministry, my sister and I were homeschooled by members of the church. I didn't go to school until the latter end of the seventh grade, and I really couldn't read. I didn't learn my vowels, nouns, or other pertinent curricula to equip me to be fully successful. When I thought of the word *noun*, it took me to the commercial of the two candy bars where they said, "Almond Joy's got nuts; *nouns* don't."

When I started school, I truly believe most of my teachers passed me because of who my parents were, not because of my understanding of the material. I asked to get a drink of water or use the bathroom every time it was my turn to answer a question or read a sentence out loud.

I went to a Baptist church with some friends shortly after I began school. In the youth class, they spelled out Bible words, and I wasn't able to even spell Jesus's name! I was really embarrassed and felt dumb, so different from normal kids.

This continued throughout my high school years, where I averaged Cs, Ds, and Fs. When it came time to graduate, I was one credit short, so summer school was needed for that last credit. This meant I couldn't walk with my class for graduation, but I did graduate in the same year.

My self-esteem was so low that one of my friends took the test to allow me to pass and get my diploma. It wasn't until many years later that God taught me how to read. I believe it was the love that my parents taught me for God that afforded me the desire to please Him. Reading God's Word allowed the Holy Ghost to assist me in reading and understanding.

I believe my parents just wanted so much of God, His anointing, coupled with the understanding that God's kingdom was close at hand, that they didn't even understand that there was a lack of correct parental responsibility. Pastoring members and preaching the Word of God became unbalanced when it came to raising the family. I believe many forget what God calls their inheritance. There is so much focus on inheriting the *kingdom* that the first preaching responsibility is often forgotten: the children. I believe that many times as preachers we forget to continue to do what we did to achieve our position in ministry, even after we obtain a higher level.

This is what many pastors tell others, yet they forget the balance on caring for their inheritance that got them to the position of pastor. They become so focused on feeding God's flock that their own children take a backseat.

It wasn't until the Lord taught me how to read that I began to have self-worth. I felt so unworthy, so ashamed, and so stupid, and this showed up in my life by me making some questionable choices, which fell right into the enemy's plan for me—the pastor's inheritance sold for the proverbial bowl of lentils! I started out as a kid praising God but in time fell to the need to be accepted and liked by others. I fell to worldly ways—even falling prey to Jehovah's Witnesses.

Don't get me wrong; I'm not talking badly about them, though some of their teachings are contrary to the Word of God. It was what my parents instilled in me that kept me searching, and when they (Jehovah's Witnesses) explained the name of God was Jehovah, I latched on to that correct tidbit.

In many ways I was sheltered yet handicapped at the same time. Giving up on our God-given inheritance (our children) is not right! Jesus said when we were yet sinners He died for us (Romans 5:8). Jesus still placed Himself on the cross, even knowing that He was hated and would be beaten, spit upon, and even disowned by those closest to Him, His disciples.

> Think not that I am come to destroy the law, or the prophets: I am not come to destroy, but to fulfill. (Matthew 5:17)

I am so glad my mother never gave up on me. She not only prayed for me, she and my dad came to my house, sat me in a chair, and went to war in prayer around and for me.

Yes, there were many things that they could have done better, but God will always turn it around for our good. I believe they should have discerned the enemy's open opportunities, which we will discuss in further chapters.

CHILDHOOD AS A PK (PREACHER'S KID)

G rowing up as a PK came with high expectations. We were to be blameless, sit properly, be well dressed, act highly respectfully, and possess preaching or teaching talents like our parents. We were to be the next generation of a long generational ministry. Ephesians 6:4 shows the qualifications of pastors, ministers, and other clergy, and the expectations on PKs fell under these qualifications that parents would need to be such leaders. I don't believe the expected behavior is out of line, but I do believe pastors forget or become so engulfed in saving the world, the members, and the church that they miss the greater attacks of the enemy on their children. As a PK, I have been attacked by the enemy more because of who my parents were in the spiritual as well as earthly realm.

Some pastoral parents worry more about how they look when the child falls than how to save the child. They will go the extra mile, drive hours, and fly to other countries to preach the Word rather than spend time with their first ministry (their inheritance).

I agree:

> For everyone to whom much is given, from him much will be required; and to whom much has been committed, of him they will ask the more. (Luke 12:48 KJV)

Spending time preaching and teaching God's Word is the calling, but we can't let our guard down when it comes to our inheritance. Family dinners, family time, family vacations, and prayer with and over your family are all paramount! Most churches pray over the pastors, but they forget the children and grandchildren. The enemy attacks our inheritance to kill pastors, so even though the pastor may be covered and lifted, they're losing their inheritance. Members will put pastors at their own tables for events, leaving the children or grandchildren to sit at other tables. This subconsciously teaches the flock that prayer or covering for your family is less or not needed. I can't picture God sitting separately from the His son, Jesus! Jesus said, "I and my Father are *one*" (John 10:30 KJV, emphasis added).

Listen, I'm not trying to negate all the good that PKs parents or leaders do, but I need to highlight that while you are saving the world, the enemy has targeted your children. As the Spirit falls upon the adults, as people run in the aisles and dance in the Spirit, the real question is, "Where is your inheritance during this time?" I believe we have gotten better over time getting the children involved with church, but when we leave the church, do we let our guard down? Because the Spirit fell and we feel so blessed, do we assume our children feel the same way?

Paul tells us the enemy is deceitful and tricky (Acts 13:10), and as a child of pastoral parents, I saw things at age five that sowed seeds in me for future time that proved detrimental—and that's how the enemy works!

The Bible tells us, "two lie down it caused a warmth" (Ecclesiastes 4:11 KJV), so if children see siblings or dating couples lying next to each other, they tend to imitate such behavior. See, the devil knows how God made us for the reproduction of humans, but we all know this kind of activity should only be done in a marital environment.

So many services, camp meetings, and conventions lasted days, and at the time it was awesome. I was able to see thousands of people praising our God and Savior. The peace and happiness were quite evident and written all over the faces of God's people. A lot of the time, I spent hours sleeping on the pew, but I believe being in the presence of God was a blessing, even if I was sleeping.

As Mom and Dad progressed stronger in their faith, they spent more and more time in the ministry helping people get to know Jesus. We had an open-door policy for members who would come over after church services to keep learning about Jesus. Some had kids, and as the adults talked about Jesus, we were outside or in our rooms playing until they finished. Sometimes I was so tired that as I tried to get my mom's attention while she was teaching, one of my sisters picked me up and rocked me to sleep.

Outings with my mom, dad, and siblings turned into big lunches with members of the church. Suddenly, everything we did was church-related. No more family vacations unless we were traveling to another convention or camp meeting. It seemed normal to sleep in our vehicle while my dad drove or sleep at one of the brethren's homes while they reminisced about God and His awesome presence during the services—and I do mean *services,* as there were several during the day.

Later in life, my father told me we attended Oral Roberts's and Jerry Falwell's service meetings. Now an adult, this was certainly a well-welcomed enlightenment! Not only was I part of God's people who heard of the miracles, I was one of the many who experienced and saw them happen! This was such an awesome time in life. I traveled with my mom and dad for ministry, until the latter half of my seventh grade year. I was then able to attend public school.

I remember attending kindergarten very briefly before home schooling, but this was before my parents began full-time ministry. Many of the trips and experiences were a safeguard. They prepared me for what God had destined me for in His Kingdom. Seeing miracles is all I know, and that's why I believe so implicitly in God and His word.

My parents did what they believed was best, but sometimes our best is unbalanced, and the good is mixed in with the bad. Oh yes, God will turn it around for our good (Daniel 3:1–30), but sometimes God's will is that we learn from our mistakes and do better. Every generation should be better, should know God better, and should be aware of the enemy's tricks and make changes.

> For whatsoever things were written aforetime were written for our learning, that we through patience and comfort of the scriptures might have hope. (Roman 15:4 KJV)

other PKs and I experienced awesome things, such as God's great moves. But we also faced the awful snares of the enemy. Some PKs were overcomers, and some did not fare so well. (We will discuss these experiences later in the book; names have been changed.) Remember the old saying, "Tell the truth and shame the devil." We are exposing the enemy and his tactics, not belittling pastors or leaders. What was meant for harm, my God will turn around for our good.

CAMP MEETINGS
AND REVIVALS

A s I mentioned in previous chapters, I experienced camp meetings and revivals that are unparalleled today. The hours upon hours of praying, worship, and singing was so intense, the spirit of the Living God was so evident that it swept through the services; brothers and sisters were just falling out in the Spirit.

Around age five, and then more so around age seven or eight, the waves of the Holy Ghost hit brothers, sisters, and even children in the congregation. People in wheelchairs literally stood up and ran the stadium field. Blind eyes opening was just an everyday occurrence, as it seemed so many regained their sight almost every time services were held (hallelujah). I was away for such camp meetings for weeks at a time, unlike today, in which most big meetings last a few days, at the most. I stood praising God with my hands lifted high, and then I woke up lying on the floor, not realizing what had just happened. I recall being so happy and feeling warmth, which now I understand was God's love!

Every Sunday we attended the church my parents had established, and it seemed like the Holy spirit showed up every time. We had teams from professional roller derby show up for services accepting God's love and salvation (see Romans 10:9). God the miracle worker was in fact working great, awe-inspiring miracles that were indisputable. More and more people were added to the church, not quite like Jesus's day of five thousand, but there were significant numbers to praise our Lord and Savior. God's people gave willingly of their resources and great amounts of time for kingdom interests. It was all about the kingdom preaching and teaching because the end was near, and we would soon see the presence of our King, Jesus. This little light of mine was shining bright, just like others; we were not going to hide it under a bushel, oh *no*!

God was doing His part and imparting the Holy Ghost, who was promised in Acts 2 by Jesus. The church was at full speed: my siblings singing, playing instruments; sinners confessing and becoming followers of Jesus; miracles—and I mean *real* miracles—were happing. God was being Glorified and His presence was established.

Now, I fast forward, and it has been many years later. My mom and dad have passed on to glory, so I'm not able to ask them about the places we visited or where we worshipped, but I thank God for His Greatness. One thing is quite interesting about how God works: I ended up in school studying theology at Oral Roberts University and finished my degrees at Liberty University (Jerry Falwell's).

WHAT IS SEEN CANNOT
BE UNSEEN

This statement is true of good and bad things. In the last chapter you got a glimpse of my experiences of camp meetings, revivals, and conventions. Memories of these miracles and worship times can never be removed from my memory. The impact of the presence of God will always be with me no matter how many years pass. The personal touch from God will be an indelible part of my existence now and forever. See, no matter what the enemy means for harm, God tells us that He *will* turn it around for our *good*! (Daniel 3:1–30).

Growing up I heard and saw school riots that my brother attended, and I visited my brother (who has passed on) in a mental institution, which affected me then and still does now. I thank God the Holy Ghost is able to keep those fears in check and give hope through the Word.

Some young children were exposed to unmarried couples expressing inappropriate affection toward each other, or seeing unmarried people sleeping in the same bed together. These could be the generational curses we all preach and pray against! Many times we blame the devil and demons, but it is a learned behavior that the enemy exploits. For example, Abraham lied about Sarah being his sister, and years later, his son, Isaac, did the same thing during his situation, which is why I believe many things are learned.

Case in point, Abraham: "And Abraham said of Sarah his wife, She *is* my sister: and Abimelech king of Gerar sent, and took Sarah" (Genesis 20:2 KJV, emphasis added).

Isaac: "And the men of that place asked him of his wife, so he said, She is my sister, for he feared to say, She is my wife; lest, said he, the men of the place should kill me for Rebekah, because she was fair to look upon" (Genesis 26:7 KJV).

If as a child you see your parents fighting, fighting with your spouse later in life might feel normal because of your experience at that young age. Some grow up without a mother or father, and without realizing it, may feel neglected and have an excessive need to be loved. Oftentimes it's not initial experiences but rather the seeds that are planted for future time that are the problem.

The Bible tells us that "the Enemy is a roaring lion seeking whom he can devour" (1 Peter 5:8 KJV).

Our children today are exposed to so much more than they were even ten years ago. The devil can put snares in place that will affect our relationships with our parents and especially with God in the future. What we experience in life just doesn't go away, even when we have a relationship with Jesus. It's the Holy

Spirit that holds these things at bay as it's not the Holy Ghost's job to take it out of us!

Paul said in Romans 7:21, "I find then a law, that, when I would do good, evil is present with me" (KJV). When we progress as Christians, the Holy Ghost helps us keep it at bay, in its right compartment, and He gives us hope that things will change and the pain of such mistakes will end (see Revelation 21:3–4).

The reason for writing this book is to expose the weaknesses in our relationships with our children, in church pastors and their inheritance. The Bible tells us in 2 Corinthians 12:10 that when we are weak, we are strong. Pastors and leaders may just be parents who fell down and got up (see the song "We Fall Down" by Donnie McClurkin). When we recognize where we have missed the mark, missed the cunning of the enemy, we are now made strong in the way that we are not deceived any longer and now can fight the enemy with our eyes fully open.

I know from experience that making mistakes is part of life, but admission only makes you better, makes you greater, and people can respect you more. I remember the mistakes of the apostle Peter, who disowned Jesus. After much remorse (and I believe asking God to forgive him), he got up and became better, not making the same mistake.

Abraham and Sarah lied because they were afraid (Genesis 20), and we read later that their son, Isaac, made the same mistake and repeated the same lie. Somehow their mistake was swept under the rug and ended up resurfacing in their son. My question is, if they had admitted this mistake and taught their child what not to do, could it have helped Isaac not repeat the same bad steps and consequences? (Roman 15:4)

We talk about sin—how bad it is and how it hurts all involved, especially how it hurts God and His feelings on the matter. We explain how it affects our present relationships as well as our eternal possibilities. But now might be the time to sit down with our children and allow them to tell us what pitfalls they have seen and what can be done to help them.

I'm drawing attention to what the enemy has done to PKs because of my experiences and other PKs' experiences, but it does apply to or affect all families in a similar way. In the next chapter we will elaborate on kids playing inappropriately while the parents are in worship or mingling with friends. We will discuss what happens while kids are in school and it clearly is an attack by the enemy. The parents are clueless many times, enjoying fun and games while the enemy is taking their inheritance.

THE DEVIL'S PLAYTIME

The names are fictitious, because we are protecting those who have told their experiences in the attempt to tell the truth; shame the devil; release the enemy's hold on them mentally, physically, and spiritually; expose holes in the armor of Christians; and open the eyes of pastors, leaders, and Christians. The goal is to expose and explain some reasons PKs fall prey to the devil's snares. Though the focus has been on PKs, these ploys can and do apply to all Christians and their children.

If you find yourself feeling certain ways after reading this book, please consider dropping to your knees and seeking the Father for change, advice, or understanding on how to help your children and other PKs. A former pastor of mine, a mentor and friend, once said the truth only offends a crook (Last Generation Version)! We have souls too; some pastors and leaders will go above and beyond for members' kids. But when it comes to their own inheritance, is it possible that their children or grandchildren can come first now or at least be equal?

But when he came to himself, he said, "How many of my father's hired servants have more than enough bread, but I perish here with hunger! I will arise and go to my father, and I will say to him, 'Father, I have sinned against heaven and before you. I am no longer worthy to be called your son. Treat me as one of your hired servants.'" (Luke 15:17–19 KJV)

The prodigal son's father was noted as showing great kindness to his worker, so the son said to just treat him like the regular servants, but we know the father went well beyond that! He ran out to him, put clothing of riches on him, and threw a party because *his son,* who was dead, was alive again! See, the father could have reasoned that the son had spent his inheritance and was no longer worthy of any more riches or favor, but that just is not how God thinks. As we know, this is a lesson for all leaders and pastors on how to react in these situations.

Following are what others have revealed and exposed so you might have a change of heart and mind when it comes to your inheritance.

Johnny

Johnny, a PK much older than thirty now, found himself at the young age of five touching a girl inappropriately in school during a movie. In speaking with him, he remembers being held by a church member and believes that a spirit jumped from this person to him.

This was the first of other inappropriate behaviors. He remembers being at a convention where this behavior happened again, while they were alone.

Listen, while you parents or pastors are enjoying the presence of God, the enemy is infecting your children, planting seeds for a rebellion to come. What is seen at an early age affects one's behavior! Demons are just waiting for the right time to attack, and if your children are left with people who have not been properly delivered, those wicked seeds are planted.

Jimmy

Jimmy, a PK, remembers hanging out with other kids during a church service. Some fondling occurred between him and another boy; this was when homosexuality was taboo. Seeds were planted that could have germinated, but *God*! Experiences like this are why I stated earlier that while the parents are dancing and singing and being filled with Jesus, the devil is not worried about them because he is stealing their children, their inheritance! Later, when the child acts out, then they want to just throw them by the wayside, and here comes the famous saying: "Didn't I teach you better?"

Others played "doctor" while the parents mixed and mingled with friends. The very ones they thought were a great influence on their son or daughter were, in fact, being used by the enemy to ultimately sow seeds that would bloom a few years later. This is how the enemy works and it's often missed.

I personally know PKs who fell away because they believed

their pastoral parents spent more time helping others, such as members, drug addicts, and alcoholics more than they did them. Yes, you have been called to save souls in this world; you were called to help dying people, but this cannot be at the expense of your own inheritance! If you treat members and sinners who come to church better than your own family or children, something is wrong. Pastors seem to have more longsuffering for others than their own children. It's not about *you*, it's about saving souls, and not only are your children souls, they are your inheritance and responsibility, entrusted to you by Jesus.

The Word tells us that the more we are given, the more the requirements will be (Luke 12:48). We must remember that the more we do, the more attacks the enemy plans. The devil attacked Job's wealth and his family first. Satan killed all of Job's children because Job was called righteous and blameless.

We are not given a spirit of fear but of power, love, and *soundness of mind*! It's time to fortify our children, who are not only *our* inheritance but the inheritance of the church. The enemy wants to kill the longevity of the generational ministry.

I ran around with my older brothers, and we, as PKs, used to break windows with rocks or chestnuts, throw eggs into traffic causing accidents, and even steal from stores. Often this was done during worship services or my parents' fellowship times with other Christians.

Yes, this seems trivial compared to the earlier examples, but it starts small and then germinates. The lack of love felt from my parents ultimately contributed to my searching for love in all the wrong places. Your inheritance is the devil's playground.

DISOWNING YOUR INHERITANCE

My fear is that we, as pastors, leaders, or full-time servants are so dialed in on saving people that we forget to fortify our own homes while we are being raped, pillaged, and taken hostage!

Our families were once our first ministry. The enemy attacks our families, our children while we are saving others, in response to our doing good works. In 1 Samuel 30, I am reminded of how David and his men were busy away at war and the enemy came into his own camp and took David's' wife and children captive. It's time to preach, teach, and save others, but we must be balanced enough to keep our own families safe. We need to balance our time to allow our own children to understand how much we love them and that we would move heaven and earth for them. We are so intent on the now that we forget that this is an endurance fight, and we are selling our inheritance for a bowl of soup.

Oftentimes we forgo vacations, family trips, and family time because we believe the church will fall prey if we are not there. Perhaps you have even had experiences of wolves in sheep's clothing (Matthew 7:15), and that's stopped you from leaving the church, even for a day, to spend time with your family. If the church cannot stand without you, something is wrong!

People are following you and not Christ. Christians who love Jesus will love Him when you are there and when you are away, rekindling and preserving your first ministry. Time with our family today has become an afterthought and not our first thought. Once the minute, hour, day, or year is gone, you can't retrieve it, buy it, or snap your fingers to get it back. I have learned from my parents, their strengths and weaknesses, which allows me to eat the meat and spit out the bones. I live by this model (*God-family-church*). No matter what, God comes first in all things, as He is the lover of my soul, the lily of my valley, and my bright Morning Star. He has shown me how much He cares by spending time with me daily. He paid the ultimate price, and this, as the Word says, is the greatest love ever (John 3:16).

We have family because that's what Jesus died for; we have no church without families! Paul said what do I have if I gain the whole world and forfeit my soul. I ask you, what do you have if you gain all of mankind at the sacrifice of your own children? Is that really God's plan, and would He be satisfied with this loss?

Jesus said:

> While I was with them, I protected them and kept them safe by that name you gave me. None has been lost except the one doomed to destruction so that scripture would be fulfilled. (John 17:12 KJV)

When I read this, I get the feeling Jesus didn't really even want to lose Judas.

Mistakes are yesterday, but we have the now to make the wrong things right! I love and appreciate my godly pastoral parents, but there were times we PKs needed help and they sent members or prayed over the phone for us, which was good ... but to help others, they spent hours and thousands of dollars traveling countless nights tending to members' problems.

May I submit: balance, balance, balance! People joke about how PKs are the worst of Christian values, but I submit that just because of the pastors' position, PKs are highlighted more than the average person. If you're going to hold PKs to a higher standard, then you should pray and help them more than the average too.

Preachers' kids are caught in the crossfire, held to that higher standard, expected to be as holy as the parents because of the parents' calling. No, I'm not making excuses for preachers' kids, as we all are called to holiness, but remember that the enemy attacks us more because of our parents' calling!

LEADERS' MISTAKES

I n my opinion, leaders do not underestimate the enemy, but we are now seeing the hole, the exposed area, the totally unprotected area in our armor. As mentioned before, most spend hours in prayer for the church; hours and days traveling for ministry; and hours visiting the sick and teaching, preaching, and upbuilding the Body of Christ.

My parents studied the Word countless hours to have fresh manna for the people of God. Yet I believe we have taken it for granted that because we are doing so much and have such a close relationship with Jesus, our children have the same cover. Just because PKs don't complain doesn't mean we don't feel rejected, unwanted, or less than. When children act out, it's usually because they are missing something or have a need not being met. Remember, "Hurting people hurt people."

Preachers' kids fall prey because of the normal need to be part of what is happening, to feel loved and not like they are an afterthought! The devil preys on this normal desire as he too knows how God made humankind. See, pastors and leaders are so busy caring for their flocks that we allow others to help raise our children, babysit, and stay with them at their homes, not recognizing that we are opening our inheritance up to spirits that are looking to attach themselves to them. We must be careful about who carries our children and what type of contact our children have with others. Please ask yourself, how many times do I hug and love members, and is it an amount equivalent with my own children?

Pastors and leaders must remember to keep that same fervent desire to raise our children in righteousness, love of Jesus, and respect of God's ways that allowed us to achieve the position; even more so after because our children are under attack even more so! The enemy attacks PKs to get at leadership, and I believe with all the duties that come with caring for the flock, clergy forget this simple, basic, and strategic tactical plan of the devil.

It's interesting that the flock follows the leadership's example, and as we all know, the flock many times are a representation of their leadership. If the pastor or leader forgets to mention, love, appreciate, or openly respect their children, the flock does the same. If you pray for the pastors, pray for the children, as they are under the same attack of the enemy. The devil attacks the family, the PKs, to cause hurt, harm, and divisions, and to cause pastors the pain that they are inflicting on the enemy by saving souls.

Growing up, I remember taking trips to department stores with my parents as they bought gifts or presents for us as children. They would buy subs for lunch as a family, and I still remember that to this day. I felt the love, the unity of being family with my six siblings, mom, and dad. We went to the park for a picnic, sometimes playing Frisbee, enjoying meats and cheese and crackers. But once ministry started full time, these short trips stopped, and vacations revolved around church meetings, campground meetings, or conventions.

We are servants of a great God, and I believe in giving my all to Him, but God doesn't exact so much that family is forgotten. Knowing God should make us want to spend more time with family, not less. It is interesting that God said of His followers that He has made us priests of Him and we shall reign with Christ.

Christ is certainly supreme, but He makes us an intricate part of reigning with Him, not separate or below Him, even though He is so much more supreme, all knowing and all powerful. Are we so holy that our children feel like we're untouchable? Being a pastor doesn't mean you are not a daddy or mommy anymore.

During wartimes, the nations protect women and children first; they are not just an afterthought. Church leaders, out of respect, set you at your own table, put you on pedestals, cook you dinners, buy you gifts, pray for you weekly, but please, remember that you are still dad and mom first. At the end of your assigned time in the ministry of pastoring, you are left with your children, and whatever relationships you have built are the ones you will live with.

God is not unrighteous to forget your works (Hebrews

6:10), but all the accolades that come with the position switch to the next pastor. When was the last time you cooked for your children, no matter their ages? Just because our children grow older doesn't mean they are not our children anymore. Who doesn't love mamma's cooking? Dad's BBQ skills?

Pastors and leaders, we have an assignment from God, but He doesn't expect us to accomplish it at the expense of our children. He requires balance.

Take your "pastor hat" off and hug your children. Tell them you love them, and tell them their worth. Speak the great things about them.

If Jesus lay down His life on the cross for them, are you willing to do the same?

Stop being all that, and be all that.

GOD'S PLAN FOR
RESTORATION

N ow, it's interesting in this passage of scripture that Paul refuses to accept payment or support. As the scripture reveals, this is the third time:

Behold, the third time I am ready to come to you; and I will not be burdensome to you: for I seek not yours but you: for the children ought not to lay up for the parents, but the parents for the children. (2 Corinthians 12:14 KJV)

We know this was for several reasons, one being that Paul wanted everyone to understand that it's God who supports him, makes the way, and receives all the credit, and no one could refute this. He was also setting the stage for all to know that it was his responsibility to care for them as his spiritual sons and daughters, not theirs as his children. Parental responsibility never ends just because you are a leader or pastor.

Lo, children are an heritage of the Lord: and the fruit of the womb is his reward. As arrows are in the hand of a mighty man; so are children of the youth. Happy is the man that hath his quiver full of them: they shall not be ashamed, but they shall speak with the enemies in the gate. (Psalm 127:3–5 KJV)

Train up a child in the way he should go: and when he is old, he will not depart from it. (Proverbs 22:6 KJV)

And, ye fathers, provoke not your children to wrath: but bring them up in the nurture and admonition of the Lord. (Ephesians 6:4 KJV)

And these words, which I command thee this day, shall be in thine heart: And thou shalt teach them diligently unto thy children, and shalt talk of them when thou sittest in thine house, and when thou walkest by the way, and when thou liest down, and when thou risest up. (Deuteronomy 6:6–7 KJV)

Pastor and Leaders, the fight is not over until it's over! What the enemy means for harm, God has promised to turn around for our *good*. Just because mistakes were made doesn't mean the family curse must continue. My pastoral parents made mistakes, but I'm living proof that God can and will use it to make your children better as time passes. The Word of God and the time you spent with your children will work in the way it was intended!

Proverbs 22:6 gives us assurance that what was planted will not depart for them (hallelujah). Be human and humble enough to admit your mistakes. Make changes now while there is yet time, for someday soon it can and will be too late. Love covers a multitude of sins, and where love is, love never fails. There is a reason that love of God is the greatest commandment and loving our neighbor as ourselves is the second. It was *love* that held Jesus to the cross on Calvary, not the nails, and not the guards. Remember, leaders and pastors, God loved you when you didn't love Him; can you do the same for your children? If you love, love, love, God will do the rest! Yes, we have to tell the truth and call sin, sin! But remember: we hate the sin, not the *person*! Especially *our inheritance*.

Pastor and leaders are people too. Pastors and leaders are parents too. Pastors and leaders are servants too. But please remember, we are moms and dads first. When I go into my prayer closet and address the God I serve, yes, He is the Almighty, the beginning and end of all, the creator of the universe, the Alpha and Omega, the all-knowing, all powerful, the miracle worker, the judge and jury, the exactor of punishment, and the God of Abraham, Isaac, and Jacob—but my first word to Him is *Abba*.

Abba, I belong to you. He is all that and so much more, but in that instant of time, my intimate relationship is *Daddy*. Oh, how much I love Him comes to my mind and heart. I'm under His wings of *love* and protection, and I just know everything is going to be all right. Our children should be better than we are if we spend the time with them, if we invest in them. We can accomplish ministry and God's calling without sacrificing our inheritance. Jesus wasn't worried that His followers, disciples, and apostles would do greater.

> Very truly I tell you, whoever believes in me will do the works I have been doing, and they will do even greater things than these. (John 14:12 KJV)

He really expected them to exceed in doing greater.

If you've lost children to this world, please keep praying and loving, and let them know you might have made mistakes. Ask them to forgive you. Remember, better is the end than the beginning. Be about every soul. If your children are still part, make an intentional move to be Dad and Mom. It's OK to be a pastor at the same time.

> To the weak became I as weak, that I might gain the weak: I am made all things to all men, that I might by all means save some. (1 Corinthians 9:22 KJV)

Go on vacation with your children, and not just because you got a surprise day or two off. Make plans like it matters! God knew you before you were born. He knew your numbered hairs and all your inward parts; you were not just an afterthought.

Before I formed thee in the belly I knew thee;
and before thou camest forth out of the womb
I sanctified thee, and I ordained thee a prophet
unto the nations. (Jeremiah 1:5 KJV)

Yes, being spontaneous is awesome, but the idea is making your PKs feel like they matter. Some churches even thank the children for sharing their parents with them, which is the right thing to do. It's a sacrifice, and this is giving honor where honor is due.

Pastors and leaders, we will do greater if our children are protected in a greater capacity. We are closing the holes in the armor by applying the scriptural thought that charity starts at home. If there is any souls that I especially want to make it into the kingdom, it is most certainly the souls of my children! What good is it that we save the whole world and forfeit our own inheritance souls? Let go and let God! The past is just that, and the future is forgiveness and love.

Depart from evil, and do good; seek peace, and
pursue it. (Psalm 34:14 KJV)

Yes, this is of great importance to keeping, mending, and reconciling with your inheritance. The peace depends on you, not just your children. We make the application but not the correct response to it.

As a minister of the Gospel, a mission traveler, and kingdom witness with my awesome wife, we have learned to spend time with our children, praying with them, listening to their complaints and dislikes. We plan vacations that are not merely the same time as the conventions or Church of God of Prophecy international assemblies. We choose to let them know that we love them, that we want to be around them and that they matter to us, just as much as preaching to others, if not more! We support their games and activities, even if we must miss church at times. (No, this is not an excuse to miss church services.)

We sometimes set aside Saturdays to drive an hour and a half to get pizza or hot wings at one of our favorite spots. It's the spending time together that's the real reason for the travel, not the pizza. We make sure the time spent in ministry, loving people, helping people is equivalent to the *quality* time spent with our children.

We have family time watching movies together with popcorn, cake, and pizza or other foods, and this is the only time they are allowed to eat in the living room. We make sure it's understood that it's a special time together as family.

We have prayer time as a family, and we make sure all our kids pray out loud because I want to hear them talking to the Father for their needs. We pray for countries, churches, tests at school, healing for their bodies, and anything that concerns them. Sometimes we pray in order from the oldest child to the youngest.

Just like family time, we have family meetings, where they can voice their views or opinions. We allow the Holy Ghost to help us, using logic and the Word to bring clarity to their feeling and thoughts. We emphasize loving each other and using patience with each other, not bulling one to view things the way we do, but understanding why we act the way we do. We show them how to love, why to love, and most importantly, to love themselves and their siblings, love us as parents, love others, and specially to love *God*.

One thing I have learned is to show love and not try to pound it into them. Bully parenting may last while they are in your house, but love lasts forever. Love will keep them from missing the mark on purpose; love will keep them when no one else is around. From my example, I strayed when I didn't feel loved, and even though the devil didn't love me, he provided a snare or used someone to make me believe and feel loved. This was just to watch me fail and fall prey to his tactics.

We make it a point to show love and express it in words, daily. We have taken quizzes on our love languages so that we all know how to respond to each other. Each child is different, so one love language used with one doesn't always work with the other sons or daughters. This helps us all make a concerted effort to meet the needs of each child and allows them to meet the needs of us, as parents. Many times we respond to each other in the way that shows our way of love, but it means nothing if that is not the language of the child or spouse. For example, I can buy my second son a gift, but he would gladly give it up in replacement of spending more time with him, because it means more and makes him happier.

Please don't sell your birthright for a bowl of lentils! Don't lose your inheritance while you're saving the world. We are not superheroes, but we are victorious and overcomers in Jesus. Just like God, we wish none to perish but for all to repent (2 Peter 3:9), and the none lost especially extends to our children. Breaking every generational curse means telling the hard truth and shaming the devil, the father of lies, the adversary, the enemy of our children's souls. The enemy comes to kill, steal, and destroy your inheritance. He wants to devour your grandchildren too because this will bring you pain, pastor or leader. No more sneaking into our camp, devil! You are exposed, and the truth will set us free.

This book was written to expose the devil and reconcile/restore.

To reconcile means

- restore friendly relations;
- cause to coexist in harmony; make or show to be compatible;
- make (one account) consistent with another, especially by allowing for transactions begun but not yet completed;
- settle (as in a disagreement); and
- make someone accept.

Restore means

- return (someone or something) to a former condition, place, or position;
- repair or renovate (e.g., a building, work of art, vehicle) so as to return it to its original condition; and
- give something (previously stolen, taken away, or lost) back to the original owner or recipient.

If you are a PK, I and others recognize and understand many of the attacks on your life. Ultimately, the enemy has targeted you as he comes to kill and steal even your birthright! I stand on the fact that hurting people hurt people, and this applies to you, my PK brother or sister.

In retrospect, I saw myself acting out because I needed to be loved, needed to know that my life mattered to my pastoral parents, and I wanted what should have been mine from the start: their attention.

The enemy preys on the fact that we are made with the innate feelings of needing to be loved. Please understand that God loves you and has not given up on you! My parents loved me, but I do understand that some things they did should and could have been done differently and better, but they did what they thought was right at the time. For you to live and be what God has called you to be, we must forgive, learn from the past, and make our future and our inheritance's future better by not making the same mistakes. Today I am in the position to change the curse, making better decisions to protect my children.

Pastors, leaders, and all Christians, please receive your children back with open arms. Sometimes we rejoice that day of their return, and rightfully so, as the Bible tells us:

> I say to you that likewise there will be more joy
> in heaven over one sinner who repents than over
> ninety-nine just persons who need no repentance.
> (Luke 15:7 KJV)

But it seems like we hold back from fully loving them; we make the decision that we will wait to see if they are truly repentant before we throw a party or help them financially. The prodigal son in Luke 15 shows the father was looking every day for the son's return, and he didn't wait until the son reached the house. The Bible says he ran to meet him far off.

> So he arose, and came to his father. But while he was still a long way off, his father saw him and was filled with compassion for him; he ran to his son, threw his arms around him and kissed him. The son said to him, Father, I have sinned against heaven and against you. I am no longer worthy to be called your son.
>
> But the father said to his servants, Bring forth the best robe and put it on him. Put a ring on his finger and sandals on his feet. Bring the fattened calf and kill it. Let's have a feast and celebrate. For this son of mine was dead and is alive again, he was lost and is found.
>
> And they began to be merry. (Luke 15:20–24 KJV)

Please remember, any other way sends mixed signals, and the enemy will exploit this as disbelief of genuine repentance. Many times the enemy will tell your child, "See? I told you that they really didn't love you. Yeah, they will rejoice over others who repent, but for you they will never trust again, let alone help you."

Remember, God will turn all the pain into praise, all the hurt into humility (1 Chronicles 7:14). Because I traveled so much with my parents during the first eleven or twelve years of my life, I missed out on schooling, couldn't read, my grades were Cs, Ds, and Fs, and I truly believe if my parents were not known as reverends or didn't own a business, the teacher should have flunked me! I became a Jehovah's Witness, smoked marijuana, abused alcohol, and had a son out of wedlock. I made bad decision after bad decision.

But one day finally came. God drew me back into the flock of His people because He had a destined outcome for me.

> No man can come to me, except the Father,
> which hath sent me draw him: and I will raise
> him up at the last day. (John 6:44 KJV)

I'm happily married with six children; a minister of the Gospel; a certified chaplain; graduate of Liberty University with dual degrees in church ministry and theology; completed a course at the School of David with certifications; called, by God, in miracle healings (I have witnessed God heal epilepsy, blindness, internal bleeding, cancer, migraines, cramps, vertigo, back pain, stomach pain, and many other infirmities). I've ministered in the mission fields of Nigeria, with plans to minister in Pakistan, Kenya, and India, doing what God has called and destined for me.

To the glory of God I am also a business owner. I say all this to help you see that God is ready to turn your pain into blessings right now. It's time for you to stand up or return home. God loves you, and He is your rewarder!